Oh, Otto!

MICHAELA MORGAN

Illustrated by Mike Phillips

OXFORD
UNIVERSITY PRESS

OXFORD
UNIVERSITY PRESS

Great Clarendon Street, Oxford OX2 6DP

Oxford University Press is a department of the University of Oxford.
It furthers the University's objective of excellence in research, scholarship,
and education by publishing worldwide in

Oxford New York
Auckland Cape Town Dar es Salaam Hong Kong Karachi
Kuala Lumpur Madrid Melbourne Mexico City Nairobi
New Delhi Shanghai Taipei Toronto

With offices in
Argentina Austria Brazil Chile Czech Republic France Greece
Guatemala Hungary Italy Japan Poland Portugal Singapore
South Korea Switzerland Thailand Turkey Ukraine Vietnam

Oxford is a registered trade mark of Oxford University Press
in the UK and in certain other countries

First published 2007

British Library Cataloguing in Publication Data
Data available

ISBN: 978-0-19-846096-1

1 3 5 7 9 10 8 6 4 2

Available in packs

Stage 9 More A Pack of 6: ISBN 978-0-19-846092-3
Stage 9 Class Pack: ISBN 978-0-19-846099-2
Guided Reading Cards also available:
ISBN: 978-0-19-915230-8

Cover artwork by Mike Phillips

Printed in China by Imago

1

Something important

The children in Class Four were busy working.

Then their teacher, Miss Underwood, said: 'I have something *very* important to tell you.'

She smiled and said: 'A new boy is coming to our class. His name is Otto and he comes from far, far away. In fact, he comes from outer space...'

The door opened and a boy came in. He looked just like the other children – but he was a different colour. He was green.

Miss Underwood told Otto to sit with Jo and Charlie and Josh. Then she looked at Jo and added, 'I want you to take care of our new boy and give him a hand if he needs it.'

‘Please, Miss,’ said Otto. ‘I’m not NEW. I’m seven and a half. And I don’t need a hand. I’ve got two hands already. Look!’

‘Oh, Otto!’ Miss Underwood smiled. ‘Just sit down and be a dear.’

Otto sat down.

Then he said, 'I don't think I can be a deer...but I *can* quack like a duck.'

He flapped his arms, like wings, and went: 'Quack! Quack! Quack!'

Charlie joined in: 'Quack! QUACK! QUACK!'

Miss Underwood smiled at Otto. 'No quacking in class!' she said.

Then she frowned at Charlie. 'Charlie!' she said. 'You know better than that! Get on with your work.'

'It's not fair!' Charlie grumbled. 'I get into trouble and that new boy doesn't!'

That's when Charlie decided he didn't like Otto. He didn't like him one bit.

2

Charlie is cross

Otto made a *lot* of mistakes.

Charlie leaned back on his chair. Otto tried to do the same thing. But *he* fell down…

…and so did all the paints.

Now Charlie was green too – and he wasn't happy about it.

Charlie got crosser and crosser and crosser.

At playtime, when Otto was in the playground, Charlie decided to scare him.

'If you stand there, you'll get eaten by a bear,' said Charlie.

'A bear! Where?' Otto screamed.

Charlie giggled. 'We keep the bear in the head's office. All Earth schools have a bear,' he went on. 'Sometimes the bear gets out… and sometimes it's hungry!'

Otto looked very scared.

3

Treasure Hunt

That afternoon the class was having a Treasure Hunt. All the children were looking forward to it.

Miss Underwood gave each pair of children the same clue.

'I want you to work in a pair with Otto,' she said to Jo.

'Work in a pear?' said Otto 'How? It will have to be a big pear. Not too juicy. We could all get sticky.'

Jo laughed. 'Oh, Otto! You don't understand anything!'

The Treasure Hunt began.

Charlie worked with Josh. Jo worked with Otto.

This was the clue that they had to follow:

'What does that mean?' said Charlie.

'I don't know,' said Josh. 'But when Miss Underwood hid the treasure last time, it was in the playground.'

'Let's go there!' Charlie said to Josh. 'Quick! We'll be first.'

Otto jumped up to follow them – but Charlie had a plan. He stuck out his foot and tripped Otto up.

'Enjoy your trip!' Charlie laughed, and ran off with Josh.

Jo helped Otto up.

All the other children ran out of the classroom and followed Charlie and Josh. They turned right, towards the playground.

Jo sighed. 'Now we're going to be last.'

'We *won't* be last,' said Otto, 'because they're all going the wrong way. Look at the clue.'

Otto pointed at the clue. 'It means we start here – at the classroom door and we don't turn RIGHT – because that would be wrong. We have to turn LEFT.'

They set off in the other direction to the rest of the children.

Charlie and Josh were looking for treasure in the playground and they were getting fed up.

'There's nothing here,' said Charlie. 'Let's look inside the school.'

They went back into the school hall, past the head's office and that's when they saw it…

'There IS a bear!' Charlie said. 'There really is!'

They ran screaming back to their classroom.

'Help! Help! We've seen a bear.'

4

Oh, Otto!

Jo and Otto had turned left and walked along the corridor.

'Look!' said Otto.

There was an arrow and it was pointing to a plant pot.

Jo picked up the pot and found a map.

There was another clue on the map.

'Let's go!' said Jo.

Jo and Otto followed the map to the school library.

Jo read out the clue again:

'Follow this map
if you want to do well.
Just look in the place
where you find a spell.'

'I understand!' said Otto. 'Look – there's a pile of spelling books. That's where we'll find a "spell!"'

'You've got it, Otto!' said Jo.

Behind the pile of spelling books, there was a box of golden coins. 'Yum!' said Jo. 'It's chocolate money!'

Back in the classroom, Jo and Otto shared out the treasure chocolate.

'But what's the matter with Josh and Charlie?' asked Otto.

Some of the other children laughed.

'Charlie and Josh thought they saw a bear!'

'A bear!' said Otto. 'Jo told me you were making up that story to scare me.'

Charlie looked ashamed. 'It wasn't *really* a bear,' he said. 'It was the head's big new coat hanging on the door...'

'But it LOOKED like a bear,' said Josh.

Charlie and Josh went bright red.

'Don't worry,' said Otto. 'Everyone makes mistakes. Have a chocolate.'

'I'm sorry I made fun of you,' said Charlie.

Charlie looked so sad that Miss Underwood felt sorry for him.

'We'll forgive you, Charlie,' she said. 'We all have bad days.'

She smiled. 'You and Josh seem to have lost your heads, today!'

'Oh!' said Otto. 'Shall I look for their heads, Miss? I'm good at finding things!'

About the author

Sometimes a name can set a writer off thinking of a story.

I wanted to call one of my characters Otto. Write it backwards and what have you got? Yes – Otto.
I thought maybe someone whose name can go backwards or forwards might be a bit different.

Maybe you could write your own story about Otto and the different things he does?